GOD'S
DIRECTION
IS ALWAYS
B E S T™

A FIVE-WEEK DEVOTIONAL

TIM WESEMANN

www.CTAinc.com

GOD'S DIRECTION IS ALWAYS BEST™

Tim Wesemann

www.timwesemann.com
ISBN 0-9754499-7-4

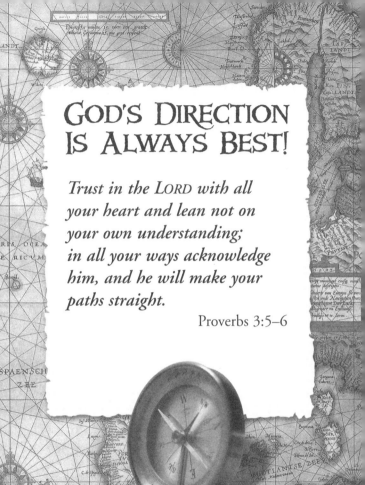

GOD'S DIRECTION IS ALWAYS BEST!

Trust in the LORD with all your heart and lean not on your own understanding; in all your ways acknowledge him, and he will make your paths straight.

Proverbs 3:5–6

DAY 1

Trust GOD from the bottom of your heart;
don't try to figure out everything on your
own. Listen for GOD's voice in everything
you do, everywhere you go; he's the one who
will keep you on track.
Proverbs 3:5–6 (THE MESSAGE)

Men and asking for directions. Isn't that like water and oil? Don't worry, men! I won't joke about or even mention the defective male direction-asking gene. Actually, it's not really defective, just often unused. Either way, I won't mention it! (Oops, I guess I just did!)

While some people never seem to ask for directions, others are not the least bit ashamed to stop and ask when confused or lost while traveling. Some people stop and ask, yet don't trust the directions they receive and decide to find their own way after all. And then there are those who will inquire about the route when they're traveling alone, but if they're with someone, forget it! They seem to think that to ask is to show weakness.

Which description best fits you? Would your answer change if you thought about these travel plans in relation to your journey with the Lord—your faith walk? your trip home to heaven?

Every turn we take, every decision, every step, every move, is part of our journey to our eternal home. Everything we do—from driving in a car to diving into a good night's sleep—is part of that journey. As God's people in Jesus Christ, we never travel alone. Our Lord is present to direct, correct, teach, forgive, and save us in our journey. He knows the best route. He leads us down the paths of righteousness, by the living streams of water, and even through—yes, *through*—the valley of the shadow of death. God's direction is always best! What great news for safe travels!

Unfortunately the sins of pride and self-centeredness often keep us from hearing and following the true wisdom and direction our divine Travel Agent wants to share with us. Though he never forces us to follow, he continually encourages us through the power of his Holy Spirit to break at a rest stop outside of Jerusalem, at a crossroad named Calvary. There he forgives us, recharges our spiritual battery, and gives us perfect directions for taking our next steps.

God's direction is always best. I pray you are blessed on the five-week journey this booklet sets out for you as you continue to walk, guided by the Spirit of the living God!

Prayer suggestion: Contemplate and pray over Eugene Peterson's translation of Proverbs 3:5–6, printed at the beginning of the devotion.

DAY 2

Trust in the LORD with all your heart.
Proverbs 3:5

It's easy to sing (and sing loudly to boot), "I am trusting thee, Lord Jesus, Trusting only thee!" Or to sing "Trust and Obey" at the top of our lungs. To sing those words is one thing. To live them and act on them is quite another.

As the world daily rains on our parade with temptations and sins, our trust sometimes turns to rust. We wonder if we can trust anyone or anything. We've been let down by plenty of people and events. Soon we begin singing to ourselves, "I am trusting me, *(insert your name here),* trusting only me!"

Our Lord calls us to trust in him—not halfheartedly, but rather with all our heart, with enthusiasm and joy! In fact, this trust is the center of true wisdom.

This may not be a new teaching for you, but maybe you've worn yourself out returning again and again to your old ways of self-trust, distrust of God's direction, which is always best. Maybe you've hurt others by trying to direct your own life or by defying God's commands outright. If so, remember that God's forgiveness in Christ belongs to all repentant sinners. At times, our Lord's forgiven people still struggle fully to trust him. We sometimes still forget that our lives are not all about us but rather all about him. He repairs broken lives and creates within us the capacity to love and trust. It's all about our Lord. While our minds and ways are finite, his are infinite. While our plans aren't always trustworthy, his direction is always best.

"I am trusting thee, Lord Jesus, trusting only thee." Singing those words is one thing. Living them out, acting on them, is quite another. But the witness of the Scripture encourages us:

- Trust in the Lord with all your heart!
- Rejoice in the calling you have received from the trustworthy Savior!
- Sing it out!
- Live it out!
- Act on it!
- Trust his forgiveness, plans, and directions—they're always best!

Prayer suggestion: Seek the full forgiveness of the Father, through his Son, your Savior, Jesus Christ, for past sins of selfishness and lack of trust in him. Then ask for courage to make amends with those whom you may have hurt in directing your own life or defying God's direction. Rejoice in the forgiveness that flows from the cross of Christ, and rely on God's promise to remember your sins no more!

DAY 3

Lean not on your own understanding.
Proverbs 3:5

Even though these words talk about leaning, I won't dust off that old joke about the farmer who named his cow Eileen because she was born with two legs shorter than the others. Nope, not going to do it—I'll spare you. Of course, if I waiver on that promise, I guess it would be called a lean waiver! Stop me! Please!

Actually, better that you stop me from leaning on my own understanding. I'm not so good with the jokes, but I'm a master at leaning on my own understanding of a situation. How about you?

I'm not the most physically flexible person in the world, but I don't think a person can literally lean on himself. You'll just make a fool of yourself trying. (Trust me on this one—I tried doing it before writing this!) Plus you'll fall down, hurt yourself, and maybe hurt someone else! You can lean on other people, but if you're putting your weight on them and they walk away, you'll fall over, hurt yourself, and maybe hurt someone else! You can prop yourself up against a building, but in some situations even that could give way, leaving you to fall over, hurt yourself, and maybe hurt someone else.

You get the picture by now. In Proverbs, our Lord tells us it's not wise to prop ourselves up against ourselves or upon our own understanding or knowledge. Tie these words with the first part of the verse, and you'll find whose understanding, wisdom, and knowledge we are to lean upon. Trust in the Lord with all your heart, the holy writer tells us. He will not give way in even the greatest storm. We have his Word on it!

The world calls for us to be independent. It warns us against depending on others. But healthy, helpful dependence is dependence on God. Make yourself at home in his love, and prop yourself up against the firm foundation of Jesus Christ. He won't let you fall!

Understand? No, no, no . . . there you go again! Don't lean on your own understanding! Lean on *his* perfect understanding of the situation!

Prayer suggestion: Pray for wisdom and understanding in the various situations in your life. Begin each petition, "Father, lead me to trust in you and not to lean on my own understanding regarding . . ."

DAY 4

In all your ways acknowledge him.
Proverbs 3:6

Small words often pack the biggest punch. The one I'm thinking about occurred in the middle of Proverbs 3:5, and it's in this portion of verse 6 as well. I'll give you another hint. This word starts with the letter *A* and rhymes with *ball*.

What a difference that word makes. Consider the difference if those words read, "in some of your ways acknowledge him" or "sometimes, when you think about it, acknowledge him."

In **all** your ways acknowledge him! Be ever mindful of the Lord and his presence, faithfully serving him. He cares about every aspect of your life!

In **all** your ways acknowledge him!
- When you hit the snooze button and when you hit the sack to snooze the night away
- When you go to work and when you work the traffic to go home
- When you pick a movie to watch and when you pick someone to watch the movie with you
  - When you play and when you pray
  - When you talk to a friend and befriend someone who needs to talk

- When you're driving and when someone's driving you . . . crazy
- When you laugh at your own gaffe and when you sigh till you cry
- When you ask for forgiveness and when you are forgiven
- When you're all alone and when you want to be left alone
- When you read a good book and when you read the Good Book
- When you acknowledge someone's presence and when you acknowledge the Lord in all your ways.

In **all** your ways, be ever mindful. Rejoice in the truth of his constant presence. Seek his face. Look for ways to serve him and share his life with others. In **all** your ways, acknowledge your Savior and his abiding presence in your life! Let his ever-present help comfort and encourage you.

Prayer suggestion: Acknowledge God's present presence and praise him for that gift!

DAY 5

He will make your paths straight.
Proverbs 3:6

As I write, my father-in-law is in rehabilitation following a bicycle accident. He broke his arm, his hip, and his pelvis. It took a couple of surgeries, hip replacement, and pelvis reconstruction to fix his breaks. Who knows how long it will take just to get him to walk again, to get his life back on course.

The interesting thing is that he was riding the bike for his health! So what happened? A small portion of the path he normally rides recently underwent some repairs, so he had to veer off onto a little detour and then return to the path. The ledge where the two paths reconnected was several inches high. The bike hit the obstacle, and he was thrown off the bike. It seemed like such a little thing, but that small obstacle has changed his life in a major way.

What a difference a single decision can make in a life. A split-second decision can lead to splitting pain, second to none. It doesn't take a boulder; even uneven pavement can pave the way for pain and change.

Obviously, it doesn't take a brain surgeon (or as in my father-in-law's case, an orthopedic surgeon) to recognize the correlation to our spiritual walk with our Savior. Satan loves to put little detour signs in our path. The world system around us makes sure our path isn't smooth or easy. And our sinful nature lures us into the self-confidence that convinces us we can make it over that little obstacle in our path. We're much bigger than that little ledge. No problem! Soon we're lying on the ground, broken with sin. How thankful we can be that we're in the best of hands— those belonging to the Great Physician, Jesus. That's how much he loves us. His cross brings us healing.

He's more than the Great Physician of body and soul; he's also the Great Road and Bridge Builder. As we acknowledge him in all our ways, he removes obstacles from our pathway and leads us back on course. The cross of Jesus is the only bridge from earth to heaven. We know it's the right, safe way because God's direction is always best!

Prayer suggestion: Consider the obstacles of trouble and temptation you continually find in your path. Ask Jesus to remove them and lead you in the right directions as you daily walk with him and his people.

DAYS 6-7 . . .
TIME FOR REFLECTION
God's Direction Is Always Best!

As I meditate on this week's theme and Scriptures, these are the things . . .

1. I want to say to my Savior-God;
2. I have learned through these devotional studies;
3. I need the Holy Spirit's help to change as I seek God's direction in my daily life; and
4. I want to be held accountable for in my faith walk.

_____

_____

_____

_____

_____

_____

_____

_____

_____

_____

_____

_____

_____

_____

GOD'S DIRECTION THROUGH HIS WORD

Your word is a lamp to my feet and a light for my path.

Psalm 119:105

DAY 8
Your word . . .
Psalm 119:105

When you give your word to someone, is it trustworthy? Always? Most of time? Some of the time? Hardly ever?

God has given us his Word. Is it trustworthy? Always? Most of the time? Some of the time? Hardly ever?

Check off the statements you believe to be true in each segment below.

My word . . .

_____ is always true

_____ is life-giving

_____ has power

_____ sometimes isn't trustworthy

_____ creates faith

_____ changes lives

_____ is completely trustworthy

_____ fluctuates—sometimes trustworthy, sometimes not

God's Word . . .

____ is always true
____ is life-giving
____ has power
____ sometimes isn't trustworthy
____ creates faith
____ changes lives
____ is completely trustworthy
____ fluctuates—sometimes trustworthy, sometimes not

How do the lists compare? The truth hurts when we honestly compare our own words with God's Word. Our faults are exposed. His perfection is obvious. God's Word is true, wise, and loving. God's Word, full of truth and guidance and love, brings life and hope. Our sinful lives and lies hurt Jesus (to the point of death—even death on the cross!), but Jesus promises an abundant, forgiven, and eternal life to all repentant sinners who place their lives in his. Go ahead. You can trust him. It's all true. You have his life-giving Word on it. (And he doesn't lie.)

Prayer suggestion: Start your prayer with the words, "Lord, where my words fall short, your Word . . ." and allow the Holy Spirit to lead your words in the direction he wants your prayer to go.

DAY 9

Your word is a lamp to my feet.
Psalm 119:105

I have very poor night vision. My family doesn't understand why I love having lights on in so many rooms at night. I've purchased many direct path nightlights, which shine specifically onto the path I am walking. Without them I'd be falling down stairs and running into chairs (as though I don't do enough of that anyway)!

It wouldn't help as much if I strategically placed nightlights pointing to the ceiling. The path is much clearer when the light shines at my feet. It's the same at the movie theater. If you enter late, there's not a spotlight shining on you to help you to your seat—you couldn't get anywhere if the light shone directly in your eyes. Theaters have lights along the floor in the aisles, so even in the dark you can see the steps you are to take.

Psalm 119:105 reminds us that God brilliantly illuminates each little step we take, as well as the full path toward our home in heaven. Even more important, the Lord cares about every step you take, every decision and every move you make, every thought you think, every second of your life. He does more than just care—he provides help, guidance, and leadership through his Word. As we allow the light of his Word to shine on our path, we find safety and wisdom in each step we take.

The Lord doesn't want you to continue hurting yourself (or others) as you trip and fall into the sinful traps of Satan. He wants to light your path, leading you safely through each day. You may experience frequent power surges as you frequent his Word, but power outages are out of the realm of possibility with Jesus, the Light of the World.

Prayer suggestion: Talk to your Lord about the upcoming steps—even the smallest ones—you take today. Remember, he may change your course, so also pray for trust as you hold on to the truth that God's direction is always best.

DAY 10

Your word is . . . a light for my path.
Psalm 119:105

Check out these facts about the sun:

- Our sun's temperature reaches 10,000 degrees Fahrenheit at the surface and 27,000,000 degrees at the center.
- The diameter of our sun is 109 times larger than Earth's; its volume is big enough to hold more than 1 million Earths.
- The sun's light takes eight and a half minutes to travel to the Earth.

What an astonishing part of God's creation we take for granted most all the time! We rely on the sun. We trust it will be there every day. We complain about its heat or the lack of it. Sometimes we even ohhh and ahhh over it, especially as we view its spectacular risings and settings.

Are your reactions to Scripture much the same? Do you marvel at its description of the Easter Sonrise or its promises for life's sunset? Do you too often take it for granted or fail to find time to read it?

Check out these facts about the Bible:

- It contains around 774,000 words in its 66 books, 1,189 chapters; and 31,173 verses.

- It is the inspired Word of God and inerrant in all it tells us (2 Timothy 3:16–17).
- It gives light to our path through life both day and night and at all times in between (Psalm 119:105).
- It especially sheds light on the truth that faith in Jesus Christ as our personal Savior is the only way to an authentic relationship with God now and forever (John 14:6).

While the first fact listed above may catch our interest, the other three truths can change our lives. When we accept the Bible as the totally trustworthy, inspired Word of God, we understand that through it, the Lord touches our lives and speaks personally to our hearts. We cherish it.

God's perfect direction, help, and salvation come to us in his Son, our Savior, Jesus Christ—the Word of God (John 1:1) revealed in the written Word of God, the Holy Scriptures. Set out to enjoy the journey! The Lord will light your way!

Prayer suggestion: Ask forgiveness for sins of apathy and complacency when it comes to allowing God's Word to be a daily light to your path. Seek God's direction for a fulfilling plan of study, meditation, and prayer regarding the light-giving, life-changing world of the Son.

DAY 11

All Scripture is God-breathed
and is useful for teaching, rebuking, correcting
and training in righteousness.
2 Timothy 3:16

Take another look at the cover of this devotional. A compass shows a traveler the direction in which he is headed. God's Word not only shows us our direction, it also alerts us when we're going the wrong way. It trains us in our faith walk.

We know what the four letters *(N-S-E-W)* on a compass represent. And our Lord also wants us to see his inspired, perfect Word as a compass useful for "teaching, rebuking, correcting and training in righteousness" (2 Timothy 3:16). Consider a new way to look at the four corners of the compass. When rearranged, they spell out *NEWS,* and this acronym can help remind us of God's good news, his promise to accompany us in our journey, hearing our prayers and guiding our steps.

Many of the Lord's answers to your prayers for guidance can be summed up in the following way as you seek his will in your decision-making. At different times he may say to you:

N—**Now!**   *(Go with God's blessings! Make his will yours! Follow him now!)*

E—**Easy!**   *(Proceed with caution. God goes with you. Watch for his continued directions along the way.)*

W—**Wait!**   *(The timing is wrong. He will reveal more down the road, as you seek his direction.)*

S—**Stop!**   *(Don't consider this. It defies God's will for his people or his purposes for you.)*

It may be helpful for you to write these out and put them in your Bible for future reference as you seek God's direction, which is always best! But even if you don't remember the NEWS acronym, remember the good news that God has provided his Word to guide you on your way through this life and into heaven.

Prayer suggestion: Pray about one or two specific decisions you are dealing with at this time. Ask the Lord to reveal Scripture verses to guide you and make his direction very clear to you.

DAY 12

All Scripture is God-breathed . . . so that the man of God may be thoroughly equipped for every good work.
2 Timothy 3:16–17

I've always felt a little sorry for Ephesians 2:10. Many people can quote Ephesians 2:8–9 but have no idea what the next verse has to say.

Sometimes the church is hesitant to talk about good works because no one wants to give the impression that the good we do saves us or in any way adds to the perfection Jesus already grants us in his cross. But by ignoring good works, by not teaching God's people to do them, too often we forget that good works are a response to God's saving grace. He has called us to do good works, not to better ourselves or our standing in his eyes, but to reflect his grace in our lives and to build up his kingdom.

Ephesians 2:8–9 beautifully reminds us that we are saved solely by the grace of God, through a Spirit-created faith, and there is nothing we can do to save ourselves. It's all about our Savior! So what does verse 10 add? "For we are God's workmanship, created in Christ Jesus to do good works, which God prepared in advance for us to do." The words of 2 Timothy 3:17 strike a similar chord. God's Word has been given to us to equip us for and direct us in every good work!

Let's take the compass letters, rearrange them to spell NEWS, and let them help us again today as we did in yesterday's devotion.

As you respond to God's grace in Jesus, consider these ways to glorify God through your life and equip others for service in his kingdom.

N—**Nurture!** *(Care for, encourage, and cherish others as ones for whom Christ died.)*

E—**Equip!** *(Build up the body of Christ! Teach! Encourage! Pray with and for others! Receive strength from his Word and share it with the world!)*

W—**Worship!** *(What joy there is in responding to God's grace, forgiveness, and salvation with a life of worship!)*

S—**Serve!** *(Just as Christ came not to be served but to serve, he calls his disciples to clothe themselves in servanthood as we love others in word and actions!)*

Prayer suggestion: Pray for God's specific direction in your life as you nurture, equip, worship, and serve.

DAYS 13-14 . . .
TIME FOR REFLECTION
God's Direction through His Word

As I meditate on this week's theme and Scriptures,
these are the things . . .

1. I want to say to my Savior-God;
2. I have learned through these devotional studies;
3. I need the Holy Spirit's help to change as I seek
   God's direction in my daily life; and
4. I want to be held accountable for in my faith
   walk.

_____

_____

_____

_____

_____

_____

_____

_____

_____

_____

_____

_____

GOD'S DIRECTION INCLUDES THE CROSS

When the days drew near for him to be taken up, he set his face to go to Jerusalem.

Luke 9:51 ESV

DAY 15

When the days drew near for him to be taken up . . .
Luke 9:51 ESV

It was the first week in November 1985. I sat in a hospital room with one of my brothers, my sister, and some of my mom's close friends. For three years my mom had dealt with breast cancer, a mastectomy, and then the pain of bone cancer. As with most things in her life, she faced this all without a husband at her side, for he had been killed in a work-related accident almost twenty-six years before.

When the day drew near for her to be taken to heaven, we gathered in this hospital room. My mom knew it was time. In fact, the day before, she somewhat frantically asked me to take her to the hospital. She knew then, it was time, although she didn't say it to me. It was as though she didn't want to die at home. As she left her bedroom for the hospital, I took another look at the picture at the foot of the bed. The painting depicted Jesus on the cross, in obvious pain. A couple of weeks prior to this, I had asked my mom how she could handle the excruciating pain she experienced from the bone cancer. Pointing to the picture, she said, "I just keep looking at him, remembering the pain he went through for me on the cross so I could be saved, and I'm able to handle it."

None of us knows what our last days will be like, but Jesus invites us to do what he did. He "set his face to go to Jerusalem." He focused on his cross and empty tomb just outside Jerusalem. We, too, can focus on that—on his suffering and death for us and on his resurrection victory.

On that November day, my mom slipped into what seemed to be a comatose state for a few hours. We waited. All of a sudden, she sat up in bed, pointed at her children, and told each of us, "I love you and I'll see you again." She lay back down and slipped back into her nonresponsive state. It wasn't too much longer, as I was reading to her about heaven from Revelation 21:1–5, that she breathed her last breath on earth. Her soul was carried to heaven. She was in the perfect presence of the one who endured excruciating pain on the cross for her so she (and all believers) could receive an eternal life—a future—without pain or sin or death.

Prayer suggestion: In your mind, picture Jesus' perfect sacrifice on the cross. Imagine, if you can, some of the pain. Realize the love. Accept his gifts of forgiveness and eternal life. Then let the Spirit's guidance form your prayers of praise and thanks.

DAY 16
He set his face.
Luke 9:51 ESV

Jesus set his face.

With conviction, the Son of Man set his face.

With great resolve, Jesus focused on what lay ahead.

For me, these words from Luke 9:51 are some of the most powerful in all of Scripture. These few words communicate so much. They paint an overwhelming mural on my heart.

Theologian Alfred Plummer notes that the original phrase, "to set the face" is a Hebraism implying fixedness of purpose, especially in the prospect of difficulty or danger.

When's the last time you did something with great resolve? Has there been a project, an event, or maybe a person on whom you "set your face"?

Perhaps I tend to be negative, but it often seems to me there is less and less true conviction in this world. Maybe that's because we've lost our sense of what truly matters. If that's the case, our Savior-God can change our focus. He can help us set our faces—and our hearts—on those things that matter eternally—his cross, his resurrection, and his ascension into heaven. Ask yourself today:

- Are my priorities out of whack?
- Is my face set on the things of the world instead of the holy things of the Word?
- Am I ready to head to the sites on which Jesus set his face?

If so, let's go . . . to the cross! Don't stand at a distance. Get up close and personal. Let his blood-righteousness cover our sinful lives as we pray: Forgive us, Lord! Change us! Renew us! Grow us! Empower us! Then let's run to the empty tomb and cry tears of joy, knowing that because he has risen, we, too, shall live! And let us watch him ascend into heaven, where he has been given all power in heaven and earth and where he has gone to prepare a place for all who by grace have set their faces and hearts on him.

Prayer suggestion: Ask Jesus to "set your face" so firmly on eternity that your life powerfully proclaims the faith of the church down through the centuries. Christ has died. Christ is risen. Christ will come again.

DAY 17
He set his face to go.
Luke 9:51 ESV

Have you ever attended a church or ministry sponsored "Advance"? Do you have any idea what I'm referring to? Most churches sponsor them, but they're usually known by a different name—retreats! There are Women's Retreats, Men's Retreats, Youth Retreats, and Couples Retreats. Why is the church continually retreating? Shouldn't we be advancing? How can we get this idea to catch on? Can't you see the bulletin insert next week reading: "Men's Advance Next Weekend! Sign up today!" People wouldn't know what to expect.

Too often the body of Christ doesn't follow the lead of the one who set his face to go to Jerusalem.
- Jesus advanced to Jerusalem. We retreat to our comfortable seats to watch from a distance.
- He carried a cross. We carry grudges.
- He was flogged. We're hardly appalled.
- He bled. We fled.
- He advanced willingly. We willingly retreat.
- He went to the cross. We don't even like going to funeral homes.
  - Pinned to a cross, Jesus cried, "Father!" Pinned down in pain, we quickly cry, "Uncle!"
    - Facing death, Jesus said, "Forgive them!" Facing much less than death, we say, "Forget it!"

In yesterday's devotion we saw that "to set the face" is a Hebraism implying fixedness of purpose, especially at the prospect of difficulty or danger.

Jesus set his face to go Jerusalem. There he would face extreme difficulty . . . extreme danger . . . and, finally, death itself. Yet he refused to retreat. He calls us to keep advancing with him, no matter what we face ahead. The journey isn't always easy, but Jesus' help is always available, always sufficient, always perfectly timed.

Advancing daily in the direction of the cross, through repentance and forgiveness, is always best, always necessary. Advancing daily in the direction of Christ's empty tomb, we receive new life, strength, and joy. Advancing forward each day toward our own arrival in God's eternal presence in heaven is a joyful certainty because of Jesus.

Even as we face the most extreme difficulty, danger, or even death, Jesus' strength leads us onward. We live in the conviction that he will empower our commitment: "I will not retreat! I will advance in the name and for the sake of my Savior, Jesus Christ!"

Prayer suggestion: List in your mind the difficulties, dangers, and maybe even the death you face. Pray about each. Ask that Jesus give you courage, wisdom, and victorious joy as he leads you toward the gold and goal of heaven.

DAY 18
. . . to Jerusalem.
Luke 9:51 ESV

Do you have any good trips planned? An upcoming vacation can bring joyful expectation into a long, frustrating day, week, or month. When you have something to look forward to, you can relax in even the most taxing times.

This week we've been considering the powerful words of Luke 9:51, "When the days drew near for him to be taken up, he set his face to go to Jerusalem" (ESV). What would happen to Jesus inside and outside the city gates of Jerusalem on a Friday Christians call "good" was hardly a vacation. But look closer at the first words of that passage. Yes, Jesus knew what was going to happen to him in Jerusalem, and still "for the joy set before him endured the cross, scorning its shame, and sat down at the right hand of the throne of God" (Hebrews 12:2). Jesus set his face on the cross, but his vision went beyond that, beyond to the time he would be taken up, when he would ascend into heaven! Beyond the hellish pain lay the heavenly gain. Our salvation was the goal beyond the goal. Love for us was his motivation. While he was on the cross, we were on his mind.

You can set your face, too, on Jerusalem and the cross of Jesus, the resurrection ground in the garden of Joseph of Arimathea, and even on your own entry into God's presence, the eternal home, made possible for you by God's grace, through faith in Jesus Christ. Keep your focus there as you

- go to work;
- go to sleep (preferably not while at work!);
- go home;
- go to a movie;
- go to the kitchen for supper;
- go to a friend's house;
- go to Bible study and church;
- go to your computer;
- go outside; and
- go on vacation.

Obviously, you get the point! Keep focused on these Jerusalem events . . . at all times! Rejoice in the vision-correcting forgiveness Jesus gives you, because he kept focused on Jerusalem and completed the goal of salvation for sinners. Heaven belongs to us because Jesus set his sights on the Jerusalem of first-century earth and on the new Jerusalem that is to come.

Prayer suggestion: Ask for eyes of faith to keep the Savior's love always before you. Ask also for grace to live a life of joyous triumph to your King, who will one day place the victory crown upon you as he carries you across the finish line.

DAY 19

I have been crucified with Christ.
It is no longer I who live,
but Christ who lives in me.
And the life I now live in the flesh
I live by faith in the Son of God,
who loved me and gave himself for me.
Galatians 2:20 ESV

God's direction is always best, though it sometimes includes the cross. While we focus on the cross of Jesus and the salvation he won for us, we also must realize that Jesus calls for us, too, to take up our cross and follow him. You may have heard those words before. In fact, you may have heard them so often that they don't have much of an effect on you anymore.

If so, maybe this question will get your attention: What is the purpose of a cross? Crosses weren't created for people to just carry around. Crosses were made for people to die on. They were invented for executions. Does that make you sit up and take notice? Since Jesus called us to take up a cross and follow him, it means he's calling us to come and die! But this dying is for the purpose of living!

Read and then reread Galatians 2:20 (printed above). Now replace the words *I* and *me* with your own name as you read it once more. Stop and let the wonder of this truth sink into your heart.

I once led a Sunday morning worship service based on the words of Galatians 2:20. I designed the first part of the service as a funeral service. I even considered having a casket present. One worship leader read a eulogy describing our lives. He also read Scriptures common in funeral services, and the congregation sang hymns appropriate to that setting. Then the tone changed to that of a victory celebration using the promise of life found in the second part of the verse. We closed with a celebration of life and of the resurrection that is—even now—ours in Jesus.

God daily directs us to his Son's cross. There we repent of our sins and allow him to crucify them with Christ. There he covers us with Jesus' own righteousness. He is our Resurrection and Life! The cross and empty tomb go together. There hope strikes a deadly blow to hopelessness. I know that my Redeemer lives! What comfort this sweet sentence gives!

Prayer suggestion: Converse with the King of heaven about the thoughts stirred up by this devotion.

DAYS 20-21 . . .
TIME FOR REFLECTION
God's Direction Includes the Cross

As I meditate on this week's theme and Scriptures, these are the things . . .

1. I want to say to my Savior-God;
2. I have learned through these devotional studies;
3. I need the Holy Spirit's help to change as I seek God's direction in my daily life; and
4. I want to be held accountable for in my faith walk.

_____

_____

_____

_____

_____

_____

_____

_____

_____

_____

_____

_____

_____

God's Direction Isn't Always Clear (to Us)

By faith Abraham, when called to go to a place he would later receive as his inheritance, obeyed and went, even though he did not know where he was going. By faith he made his home in the promised land like a stranger in a foreign country; he lived in tents, as did Isaac and Jacob, who were heirs with him of the same promise. For he was looking forward to the city with foundations, whose architect and builder is God.

Hebrews 11:8–10

DAY 22
By faith . . .
Hebrews 11:8

Faith is a God thing.

Faith is a gracious, God-given, God-glorifying, good thing!

- By faith in themselves, people have done some remarkably harmful things.
- By faith in others, people have often been remarkably disappointed.
- But by faith in Jesus Christ, people have done remarkable things as God's Spirit worked through them.

By Spirit-created and Spirit-directed faith in Jesus Christ and by his grace . . .

- the Schmidt family started homeschooling.
- Bob talked to his boss about Jesus.
- Judy changed jobs to better provide for her children.
- the Kenyon's moved to another state as the Lord led them.
  - Delton changed careers and went to the seminary.
  - Roy had surgery.

- Bruce was given a smile to wear from sun up to sun down.
- John began tithing.
- Mark invited his neighbor to church.
- Sean and Brenna went on a mission trip.
- Ed took care of his wife, who was wheelchair bound.
- the Grabs adopted children from Russia.
- Steve and Diane started a new business.
- Billy started a Christian band.
- Rick and Tracey joined a small-group Bible study.
- Amanda and Josh started a family.
- Dave received the gift of heaven following his heart attack.
- Add your own name and grace-given gift here:

_____

Faith is a God thing.

Faith is a gracious, God-given, God-glorifying, good thing . . . for "no one can say 'Jesus is Lord,' except by the Holy Spirit" (1 Corinthians 12:3).

Prayer suggestion: Thank the Holy Spirit for the gift of faith, and then with the disciples pray, "Increase our faith!" (Luke 17:5).

DAY 23

By faith Abraham,
when called to go to a place
he would later receive as his inheritance,
obeyed and went.

Hebrews 11:8

It's easy to go with the flow, to follow the crowd, to ride the wave, to collapse under pressure, to move with the groove, to run with the wind, to . . .

But those aren't always the places God leads his people. He often calls his faithful people to go against the flow, to walk against the crowd, to fight the current, to stand strong under pressure, to move to a different groove, to run against the wind, to go places with Abraham-like faith, to go with God.

Is God calling you to special service in his kingdom? to make a change in your life? to seek forgiveness or to forgive? Are you willing to go with God when he calls and directs you? Does that thought intimidate you? motivate you? cause doubts to surface? confuse you?

Do you struggle to know when God is calling you to act or to stay still? Do you truly seek his direction when you come to a crossroad, or do you hope he'll write the answer on the wall in true Belshazzarian style (Daniel 5)?

First of all, I'd say it's often good to struggle with a decision; the struggle many times develops in us confidence in God's calling. But make sure your actions aren't based on whims, emotions, or the poll you take among your friends. We're talking about a *divine* calling to act. God's speaking. God's leading. God's calling.

God wants us to seek his direction, to seek his face, to seek his perfect will. He's not hiding his will. He won't disguise his voice when he calls. He wants us to know his ways and to walk in them. Search out Scripture. Open up in prayer, but remember to listen and look for his answer. Seek out the advice and counsel of Christians also walking in God's direction.

As you are open to God's leading, remember what Abraham and so many others have found; the direction in which God leads may follow a road less traveled or may fall along a path you've never noticed before. He may call you to go against the flow, but if he does, know he goes with you as your defender, your strength, your victorious Lord! It's time not only to seek his direction, but in trust to obey his call. Hold on (to Jesus) for the ride of your life! Go ahead . . . go with God! He goes with you!

Prayer suggestion: Totally submit yourself to God's calling and direction. WARNING: This could change your life . . . for the better! Seek his face! Search Scriptures! Attune your ears of faith to his call!

DAY 24

Abraham . . . obeyed and went, even though he did not know where he was going.
Hebrews 11:8

Definitions and dictionaries go together—except when it comes to a definition of faith. That's when one turns to Hebrews 11:1: "Now faith is being sure of what we hope for and certain of what we do not see."

You can see where the term "blind faith" comes from after reading that definition. Let's challenge that term— not Scripture's definition, but the term "blind faith."

Hebrews 11 overflows with examples of people who, some might say, stepped out in blind faith. But a closer look shows they stepped out with a "perfect vision faith." Don't you want to step out into each day and face every decision with perfect vision faith? That's what you're doing every time you move in step with God's direction! It's not blind faith if God is leading! He sees around every corner, over every mountain, and through the heavy fog and the clouds that block our view. The eyes of the almighty God have already seen your future. He's already inhabiting that future. Moving into that future, then, is anything but blind faith! With our will aligned with his, we step out in perfect vision faith, the faith that trusts what *he* sees and faithfully goes where *he* leads. We cling to his promises and presence as we follow with confidence.

Hebrews 11:8–9 describes Abraham's defining faith moment. God called and Abraham obeyed—even though he did not know where he was going. God pointed, and Abraham packed. God spoke, and soon the oxen were yoked.

God altered Abraham's plans, so Abraham built an altar for worship. God blessed Abraham, and Abraham became a blessing.

Abraham didn't step out in blind faith. He moved with perfect vision faith because God's Spirit moved within him. He packed his belongings because his heart belonged to the Lord. He knew God knew what he was doing.

Are you standing in awe of Abraham's faith and Abraham's God? Then remember that the God of Abraham is our God and Savior. And the Spirit who created perfect vision faith in Abraham will create the same kind of faith in you!

Even though we may not always know where we're going, we know for certain God's direction is always best!

Prayer suggestion: Ask for confidence to know God's Spirit has created perfect vision faith within you. Surrender your heart, moving in the direction Jesus leads—even if you can't see where you're going!

DAY 25

By faith [Abraham] made his home in the
promised land like a stranger in a foreign
country; he lived in tents, as did Isaac and
Jacob, who were heirs with him of
the same promise.

Hebrews 11:9

By faith, my grandparents moved to Brazil not long after the turn of the century. It was 1900, and my grandpa had graduated from the seminary. God had called him to serve as a missionary in a region of southern Brazil. My mother and her eight brothers and sisters would be born in Brazil, making their home in this foreign country. You can imagine that conditions the first few decades of the twentieth century weren't first class, especially for a poor missionary family.

I've been told my grandfather had fourteen preaching stations throughout the region. He rode on horseback to some, paddled through rivers to more, and walked to still others. My mom told me he would be gone for three months at a time—visiting these fourteen communities, sharing the Gospel, encouraging the established churches, baptizing new believers, and visiting the sick and dying.

By faith my grandparents, my mom, and their other children made their home in the land of Brazil, like strangers in a foreign country. My grandfather,

I'm sure, lived in tents at times, like Isaac and Jacob, who were heirs with him of the same promise.

One of my mom's brothers returned to Brazil later to serve as a pastor for the rest of his life. And one hundred years after grandpa served in Brazil, two of his grandsons currently serve as pastors in that country.

Oh, the things God can do through his people from generation to generation! If you think you have no idea what it's like to actually live in a foreign land, think again. That's where you live right now! God has called us to be missionaries right where we live at this moment. He calls us to share the Gospel, to visit the sick, to encourage his people, and to baptize all nations. He calls us to do all that and more in a foreign land.

You do realize that the place God has planted you right now isn't your home, don't you? You're on a mission trip! Your permanent address is on Grace Street in the country of Heaven. When will we move there? In God's time.

Meanwhile, we can rejoice that along with Abraham, Isaac, Jacob, my grandparents, my mom, and all God's other faithful servants, we are heirs of the same promise of heaven.

Prayer suggestion: Give thanks for the Christian pioneers from previous generations that blazed a trail for you. Pray that by faith you will share the Gospel faithfully with the next generations.

DAY 26

For he was looking forward to the city with foundations, whose architect and builder is God.

Hebrews 11:10

Lord, give me eyes of faith that look beyond the hellish conditions around me to see the gift of heaven, given without conditions by my Savior.

Lord, give me eyes of faith that look beyond my enemies so I can see the victory you've won for me.

Lord, give me eyes of faith that look beyond the pile of rubble at my feet so I can clearly see the architect and builder of my faith.

Lord, give me eyes of faith that look beyond my fears to gaze upon the Prince of Peace.

Lord, give me eyes of faith that look beyond all that crosses my path through life so I can focus on the cross of your Son who has brought me life.

Lord, give me eyes of faith that see beyond my temporary earthly home so I may fix my sight on my permanent home, heaven.

Lord, give me eyes of faith that look beyond the sin and guilt of my past so I may fix my eyes on the present and future truth of your Word, which tells me there is now no condemnation for those who are in Christ Jesus, the forgiving one.

Lord, give me eyes of faith that look beyond doors that have been closed in my face so I may face the door of eternal life, which you have opened for me.

Lord, give me eyes of faith that look beyond the guidance of the world so I may follow in your direction, which is always best.

Lord, Abraham was looking forward to the city with foundations, whose architect and builder is God. My heart desires eyes of faith that do the same.

Thank you, Lord Jesus!

Prayer suggestion: Go back to the devotion and pray the words instead of just reading them.

DAYS 27-28 . . .
TIME FOR REFLECTION
God's Direction Isn't Always Clear (to Us)

As I meditate on this week's theme and Scriptures, these are the things . . .

1. I want to say to my Savior-God;
2. I have learned through these devotional studies;
3. I need the Holy Spirit's help to change as I seek God's direction in my daily life; and
4. I want to be held accountable for in my faith walk.

_____

_____

_____

_____

_____

_____

_____

_____

_____

_____

_____

_____

_____

GOD'S DIRECTION LEADS TO HEAVEN

Therefore, since we are surrounded by such a great cloud of witnesses, let us throw off everything that hinders and the sin that so easily entangles, and let us run with perseverance the race marked out for us. Let us fix our eyes on Jesus, the author and perfecter of our faith, who for the joy set before him endured the cross, scorning its shame, and sat down at the right hand of the throne of God. Consider him who endured such opposition from sinful men, so that you will not grow weary and lose heart.

Hebrews 12:1–3

DAY 29

*Therefore, since we are surrounded
by such a great cloud of witnesses . . .*
Hebrews 12:1

Envision attending a huge parade down Main Street, USA, on Veterans Day. Picture thousands of soldiers marching down that street, humbled by the cheering crowd that surrounds them, honoring them and thanking them for their service. The service men and women have tears in their eyes, memories in their minds, and encouragement in their hearts.

Now flip the characters in that mental picture around. You are mixed in with the crowd walking on the street. Lining the streets are scores and scores of veterans. They begin to clap as you walk by. Then they cheer . . . loudly! Many shout out words of encouragement and guidance. Feeling their support, you accelerate your walk to a run. You're empowered and energized, eager to keep moving on the path. Your focus turns from the veterans on the roadside to what lies ahead.

Like an athlete in the middle of an event, you hear the crowd. Aware of its support, you appreciate its encouragement. At the same time, you so intently focus on what's ahead that you soon almost forget the crowd.

In truth, you do walk along that street. Veterans of the faith cheer you on by the faithful witness they've left embedded in your mind and the words of encouragement they've written on your heart! Jesus blazed the trail, they helped clear the path, and now you carry on.

If you've ever wondered how you made it through a difficult situation, survived a battle with an enemy, or drew up strength to go when life landed on your heart with both feet, the answer lies in plain view. You live surrounded by God's faithful people. Some have gone before you, and the witness of their words and their lives encourages you:

- The teacher who served with a heart like Jesus
- Family members who cared about your faith
- The neighbor with a Christlike attitude
- Your faith-filled coach
- The lady who sat behind you at church
- The salesperson at the corner store
- Your Christian letter carrier who prayed for you every time he left you mail
- So many others

You're surrounded—by Christ's love and the love of Christ's people! Carry on!

Prayer suggestion: Thank God—for the veterans of the cross who surround you by their past witness and for those whom Jesus is still using today to lift you up in prayer and encourage you in your faith walk. Pray that God directs you also as a witness of his grace in the lives of others.

DAY 30

Let us throw off everything that hinders
and the sin that so easily entangles,
and let us run with perseverance
the race marked out for us.

Hebrews 12:1

A man walked through an airport terminal carrying
two very large bags. They were quite heavy, so he set
them down as he took a break and checked the time.
While he looked at his wristwatch, a man standing next
to him began to admire it. "That's a great looking
watch," the man said. "It seems very unique."

"It's one of kind," the traveler responded. "It tells me the
time, not only here, but in five other time zones as well.
Plus, it gives the current temperature, the latest sports
scores, and the up-to-the-minute news headlines from
any city in the world."

"That's amazing!" the other man said, stunned. "I'll give
you five hundred dollars for it right now." The traveler
shook his head and laughed.

"How 'bout a thousand dollars?"

"I couldn't," the man insisted.

The other man wouldn't give up. "Five
thousand?"

The owner of the watch paused and thought before responding. "It is unique, but that's a lot of money. Okay. I'll sell it to you for that." He took the watch off his wrist and handed it over. As the buyer started to walk away, admiring his new purchase, the traveler picked up the two heavy bags beside him and yelled, "Wait, sir, you forgot the batteries!"

Time on earth is precious, no matter how you measure it. Our Lord intends that we invest the time he has given us, enjoying him and bringing him glory for all he's done for us in Jesus. Some folks, though, insist on lugging around burdens of guilt and worry.

What extra baggage weighs you down today? Your sins? Jesus paid the price for them when he died on Calvary's cross. Your problems? Jesus invites you to cast all your cares on him, knowing that "he cares for you" (1 Peter 5:7).

It's time to get rid of the baggage—you're free to run as fast as you can to give God the glory and others your service.

Prayer suggestion: Truly sorry for your sins, confess them to Jesus. Then receive his complete forgiveness, along with his promise to remember your sins no more (Hebrews 8:12). Finally, take off running (without the baggage), fulfilling whatever purposes he has for you!

DAY 31

Let us fix our eyes on Jesus,
the author and perfecter of our faith.
Hebrews 12:2

Days 16 and 17 of this five-week devotional led us to
the powerful words of Luke 9:51: "[Jesus] set his
face to go to Jerusalem" (ESV). Jesus fixed his eyes on
the place of his crucifixion, resurrection, and ascension.

Jesus fixed his eyes on what was in store for him, because
from all eternity he had determined that through his
death, all who trust in him as their Savior would be
justified—declared not guilty—before God the Father.

Sin skews lives—makes them ragged, misaligned, ugly,
unacceptable. Jesus Christ, the author and perfecter of
our faith, stands without sin before the Father in our
place and says, "Judge these children of yours, Father,
according to my perfect life. They are no longer guilty. I
paid the debt of their sin for them!"

Do you realize the enormity of that truth? From the
cross, just before he died, Jesus cried out, *"Tetelestai!"*
This Greek word, pronounced "tuh **tell** uh sty," means
"it is finished" or "paid in full." He cried out to
his Father that the punishment for our sins was
paid in full! Our debt is cancelled.

That was Jesus' focus during his life on earth. He fixed his eyes on Jerusalem. Now he calls us to fix our eyes on him. How? As we study his Word and pray over it, he keeps on realigning our focus. We gain encouragement from other believers who also have their eyes fixed on him and seek to do his will.

Jesus! The author and perfecter of our faith. Fix your eyes on him and his mighty love for you!

Prayer suggestion: Use your Bible to find Hebrews 12:1–3. Pray these words, personalizing them. For example, "Therefore, since I am surrounded by such a great cloud of witnesses, let me . . ."

CHE

DAY 32

*. . . who for the joy set before him endured
the cross, scorning its shame,
and sat down at the right hand of the throne
of God.*

Hebrews 12:2

Okay guys, is it possible for us to imagine we're
pregnant? Is that too much of a stretch? (No pun
intended!) Now this stays between us—it doesn't leave
this devotion, *comprendo?* We'll be the laughing stock of
the men's softball league if this leaks out!

Here's the deal. I thought and thought of a way to put
the words from Hebrews 12:2 (above) into terms we all
would find more familiar. I don't want you to think that
Jesus felt some masochistic joy as he looked toward the
immense pain and agony of the crucifixion. There was
no joy in the pain, suffering, and ridicule he endured.
The joy came in the end result. Jesus looked past the
cross and saw the joy of accomplishing salvation for us.
He would find joy in completing his work on the cross
and soon afterward being seated in the place of honor at
the right hand of the throne of God.

So let's get back to this pregnancy thought. If
you were pregnant, you wouldn't look forward
to the actual pain of childbirth. In fact, you

could probably hardly bear it. (Okay, maybe you could, but I don't think *I* could!) But why then would you go through with it? For the same reason women go through it—for the joy of holding the miracle of a newborn baby, a child sent by God, entrusted to your care. Nothing equals that experience. Those who endure the birth process keep their focus on the joy that lies at the end of the ordeal.

That's what Jesus did. He kept his eye on the new, resurrection life that would follow! That focus kept his joy alive, despite what he faced. Your new life kept joy pumping through his veins, even while he bled and died for the forgiveness of your sins and the salvation of your soul.

Did the pregnancy analogy help? It was a long shot, men, but you never know. (And the prophet Jeremiah once used it in another context—Jeremiah 30:6!)

May Christ's joy be yours through the birth pangs of life in this sinful world, until you experience perfect joy in the resurrection life of heaven because of your rebirth through the Holy Spirit.

Prayer suggestion: Pray for joy—the kind only Jesus can give. (Peace is also available—in just your size.) Allow Jesus to adjust the focus of your eyes of faith to look forward to the day you receive his gift of heaven.

DAY 33

Consider him who endured such opposition from sinful men, so that you will not grow weary and lose heart.
Hebrews 12:3

"*Consider him* [Jesus Christ]." That's more than an encouraging thought; it's important for us to put those words into action, especially if any of the questions below describe you.

Feeling abandoned? *Consider him* who walked alone to his death while his disciples abandoned him.

Feeling bitter? *Consider him* who endured bitter sufferings and death so forgiveness would join him at center stage in our lives.

Feeling like people are trying to pin you down for an answer? *Consider him* who, while pinned down to a cross, answered sin, death, and the devil with a resounding, "You are defeated!"

Feeling overwhelmed? *Consider him,* the Lamb of God who has taken away the sins of the world—a lamb led to the slaughter.

Feeling lost? *Consider him* who left his home in heaven to come to a sinful world to find and save you.

Feeling that death may lurk right around the corner? *Consider him* who walked through death for you so that whoever believes in him will live, even though he dies, and that whoever lives and believes in him will never die (John 11:25–26). (Do you believe this?)

Feeling opposition from every side? *Consider him* who endured intense opposition from sinful men so that you will not grow weary and lose heart.

Consider him. Why? So that you will not grow weary and lose heart! *Consider him* and all he went through. That, as Eugene Peterson writes in THE MESSAGE (Hebrews 12:3), "will shoot adrenaline into your souls!"

Point me in that direction, Jesus! Invigorate my faith! Lead me and I will follow! I know and trust that your direction is always best!

Prayer suggestion: Praise God for his gift of Jesus, who has directed you to a new life in him—an abundant, holy, and eternal life. Praise him also for his pure grace that surrounds and enfolds you in Jesus. That grace will not take you where his power cannot defend and support you . . . for his direction is always best!

Days 34-35 . . .
Time for Reflection
Trusting God's Direction and Promises

Reread Proverbs 3:5–6 and Hebrews 12:1–3 slowly as you reflect on the theme *God's Direction Is Always Best.* (See pages 63–64.) Then think about the truths that the Holy Spirit has impressed upon your heart as you've studied this text in depth the past few weeks. Also pray about how you might share them with someone.

_____

_____

_____

_____

_____

_____

_____

_____

_____

_____

_____

_____

_____

_____

_____

_____

PROVERBS 3:5-6

THE MESSAGE

*Trust GOD from the bottom of your
heart;
don't try and figure out everything on
your own.
Listen for GOD's voice in everything
you do, everywhere you go;
he's the one who will keep you on track.*

HEBREWS 12:1-3
THE MESSAGE

Do you see what this means—all these pioneers who blazed the way, all these veterans cheering us on? It means we'd better get on with it. Strip down, start running—and never quit! No extra spiritual fat, no parasitic sins. Keep your eyes on Jesus, who both began and finished this race we're in. Study how he did it. Because he never lost sight of where he was headed—that exhilarating finish in and with God— he could put up with anything along the way: cross, shame, whatever. And now he's there, in the place of honor, right alongside God. When you find yourselves flagging in your faith, go over that story again, item by item, that long litany of hostility he plowed through. That will shoot adrenaline into your souls!